Original title:
Inside the Quiet Walls

Copyright © 2025 Creative Arts Management OÜ
All rights reserved.

Author: Arabella Whitmore
ISBN HARDBACK: 978-1-80587-008-1
ISBN PAPERBACK: 978-1-80587-478-2

A Chamber of Silent Hopes

In corners dim where shadows play,
A cat naps loud, yet dreams away.
With every purr, the dust does rise,
As squirrels plot their great disguise.

The clock's tick-tock, a steady beat,
A mouse holds court, a royal seat.
With tiny snacks, he serves his kin,
While hidden laughs ring from within.

The slippers roam, they dance in pairs,
Like giggling ghosts on wooden stairs.
They twist and turn, a clumsy waltz,
Whilst socks conspire, who knows the faults?

So here we dwell, where whispers greet,
And silent hopes find joy discreet.
Among the fun in hushed disguise,
Laughter rises, wise and spry.

Echoes of Solitude

In the room where socks all fight,
The TV hums a tree of light.
Dust bunnies dance in a whirl,
As I ponder, should I twirl?

The chair claims me, like a throne,
While the fridge mocks me, all alone.
With leftover pizza, quite a feat,
In the battle with my sleepy feet.

Secret Gardens of Silence

Here I sit with my old cat,
He gives me looks like, 'What's that?'
A squirrel's gossip brings a laugh,
While the sun shines, I'll take a nap.

The weeds whisper like old friends,
And the garden gnome just pretends.
As my plans to weed fall apart,
I'll make art from this lazy art.

The Refuge of Forgotten Thoughts

In the attic, old hats line the wall,
Each one remembers a funny fall.
They tell tales of wobbly hair,
And of spilled juice, but I don't care.

The dust motes float like tiny dreams,
Where laughter bursts and sunlight screams.
A long-lost toy will make me grin,
In this realm, where I always win.

Hush of the Hidden Corners

Under the stairs, there's a surprise,
A jumble of shoes and board games wise.
They plot an escape with giggles loud,
While I sip tea, feeling quite proud.

A shadow lurks and gives a cheer,
For who knew silence could bring such cheer?
The clock ticks slow, with a gentle chime,
In hidden nooks, laughter steals the time.

Hidden Corners of the Heart

In the nook where socks unite,
A solitary shoe takes flight.
Crumbs of secrets, crumbs of sweets,
Dance with dust where laughter meets.

A cat that plots a master scheme,
To catch the light, that lazy beam.
And in the shadows, giggles play,
Where daydreams frolic, come what may.

Shadows Woven into Memory

Footprints in the silly fog,
Coffee stains on an old log.
A hat that never fits quite right,
Pretends to fly and takes a bite.

Old tales flutter like a kite,
Chasing shadows through the night.
A wink from ghosts, a playful tease,
Memory giggles in the breeze.

Where Quiet Dreams Take Flight

Pillows whisper silly schemes,
Where snoring joins the daytime dreams.
A bunny hops on clouds so high,
As laughing stars twinkle and sigh.

Sweet socks sing in a sock parade,
Where socks go missing, laughter's made.
Each pocket hides a joyful jest,
In the corners of a cozy nest.

The Calm of Fleeting Time

Tick-tock goes the clock with glee,
As minutes play hide and seek with tea.
Cookie crumbs, a tasty trail,
Leading to the legend of the snail.

A dance of shadows, a cheeky yell,
As time's on break, under its spell.
It giggles softly, tiptoes near,
Winking at our joyful cheer.

Where Time Stands Still

In a room where clocks take naps,
The pendulum's lost all its maps.
Bored cats chase shadows on the floor,
While the drapes gossip, 'What's a door?'

Dust bunnies hold their grand ball,
With chairs that creak and walls that squall.
As laughter echoes from a past so bright,
The floorboards chuckle at the night!

The Heart's Hidden Chamber

A drawer full of secrets, grand and wide,
Where mismatched socks and dreams reside.
The whispers of old love notes flit,
As I count my snacks—now, which to split?

Old teddy bears play poker at noon,
While the fridge hums a tuneful tune.
Laughter bubbles in the air, it seems,
As I search for lost and forgotten dreams.

Silent Stories Unfold

The walls are packed with laughter's dust,
Each crack a tale, sparking trust.
A spider spins a web of jest,
As the couch proclaims it's time to rest.

Light bulbs flicker like they want to chat,
With echoes of conversations—how 'bout that?
A calendar hangs, all the days are gray,
Yet somehow, magic finds its way.

The Calm Between the Cracks

Beneath the floor, a parade of mice,
Dance to the rhythm of crumbs—how nice!
The vase holds grudges, glaring at dust,
While the books all whisper in secret trust.

A ticklish breeze sneaks through the screens,
Tickling the corners of forgotten dreams.
In silent chaos, joy runs wild,
As time plays tricks, much like a child.

Unseen Connections

A cat on a shelf, how high can it get?
Eavesdropping secrets, don't pay any debt.
The goldfish conspires, behind its own glass,
Witty remarks, as the hours they pass.

The plants gossip softly, their leaves touched by fate,
While socks in the drawer hold a secret debate.
The toaster's quite smug, the kettle's in line,
Sharing some laughter over breakfast divine.

Reflections in the Dust

A shadow waltzes, just out of reach,
With squeaky old shoes, it's got quite the speech.
The dust bunnies whisper, with mischief at play,
Plotting to dance on the floor, come what may.

Mirrors are laughing, they know all your tricks,
While clock hands tick-tock, unleashing their kicks.
The rug hides a story, a tale of its own,
In the quiet of corners, where mischief is sown.

Beneath the Hushed Canopy

The ceiling fan spins, a slow waltz in air,
While curtains conspire, their secrets they share.
A raccoon in a hat thinks he runs the whole show,
With jokes about squirrels that only they know.

The remote plays coy, hiding under a seat,
While sneakers plot mischief, you'll be in for a treat.
A funny old story lies under each floor,
As the fridge hums a tune that you can't help but adore.

Murmurs of the Unspoken

The toaster's a bard, singing bread into gold,
While the fridge holds its secrets, so spicy and bold.
A chair creaks with laughter, it knows all the views,
As dust motes keep dancing, it's all the right cues.

The walls have their whispers, spinning tales out loud,
Of socks that go missing, who'd think they're so proud?
As spoons gossip softly, about their last stir,
In the backdrop of laughter, all things occur.

Serenity Surrounded by Stillness

In the corner, a cat takes a nap,
Dreaming of fish with a quirky flap.
A pig's snore echoes with comic flair,
While the goldfish stares, unaware of care.

The clock ticks loud, but no one's awake,
A sleepy dog contemplates a big cake.
Sunlight filters through dusty panes,
While squawking birds play silly games.

Potted plants stretch, reaching for light,
But the cactus pokes, ready to fight.
Laughter bubbles under breath like a stew,
In this sanctuary, madness feels new.

Everyone's quiet, but giggles ensue,
At the faintest sounds made by a shoe.
Here joy hides in each playful glance,
A comedy lives in this stillness dance.

The Space Between Heartbeats

Tickle the silence, it starts to grin,
A potato rolls with a mischievous spin.
Laughter bubbles in the gaps of air,
While a sock puppet gives a curious stare.

Heartbeat whispers, it's all in tune,
A cactus serenades to the light of the moon.
Every pause holds a joke waiting to bloom,
And echoes seem to giggle throughout the room.

The clock breaks the quiet with a loud chime,
But we dance in circles, lost in the rhyme.
Two left feet stumble, but who's keeping score?
In this silent ballet, we can't help but roar.

Rusty hinges creak in time with a beat,
A mouse fiddles tunes with tiny little feet.
In the stillness, joy wiggles and glows,
A secret party where hilarity flows.

Whispers of the Lost and Found

In the attic, treasures breathe with ease,
A mismatched sock giggles in the breeze.
Old board games stacked, seldom to play,
But their stories dance brightly in a sleepy sway.

A half-baked hat laughs at its fates,
While a chair ponders its past debates.
Two spoons argue about who stirs the tea,
In this quiet rumble, it's all jubilee.

Faded maps lead to nowhere at all,
But they chatter of places where shadows brawl.
A dusty globe spins tales so round,
Of lands unexplored and lost, but found.

Every creak is a chuckle, a cheerful sound,
In this hidden space, whimsy is crowned.
The corners hum with joyous delight,
As laughter finds a home in the night.

Serenity's Hidden Spaces

In a cluttered nook, a secret unfolds,
Where a forgotten toy spins some tales of old.
A rubber duck dreams of grand escapades,
While a shoelace winks, joining in charades.

An old chair whispers secrets of rest,
While dust bunnies plot their next great quest.
A butter dish shines brightly in the light,
As a lonely spoon giggles, trying to take flight.

The shadows dance, weaving stories anew,
Chasing the echoes of laughter so true.
Hidden in corners, serenity waits,
For joy to burst forth through the enchanted gates.

With every tick of the clock on the wall,
Life's silly antics become the great call.
In these secret places where laughter is found,
The heart finds its rhythm, a joyful sound.

Memories Encased in Silence

Dust bunnies host a grand ball,
They twirl around, but never fall.
Old socks converse without a sound,
Telling jokes in layers unbound.

The clock ticks slow, it cracks a grin,
It knows the secrets held within.
A chair squeaks laughter, what a sight,
As shadows dance in the soft light.

The cat plots mischief from the shelf,
Staring hard at the dust like an elf.
Each creak of wood, a subtle cue,
For stories whispered just to few.

Laughter's trapped in wallpaper so bold,
A tapestry of stories told.
In corners, memories intertwine,
A comedy of life so divine.

Fading Footsteps

Footsteps echo, then they fade,
Like jokes told that never stayed.
The floorboards moan a sneaky tune,
As if they hide beneath the moon.

Each step recalls a funny tale,
Of mismatched socks and shopping fails.
The hallway chuckles, damp and bright,
With whispers of a past delight.

A flip-flop's joke goes on repeat,
As sneakers shuffle to the beat.
Remember when the cat took flight?
The laughter bursts into the night.

Ghosts of giggles linger near,
As we recount our past frontier.
Lost memories in every crack,
Well-timed jokes bring the laughter back.

The Language of Solitude

Solitude speaks in giggles low,
With pillows giving the best show.
A mirror winks, a playful tease,
Reflecting moments that aim to please.

The kettle hums a hoppy beat,
Whistling tunes, oh what a feat!
Spoons chat softly, spinning tales,
Of adventures where laughter sails.

A ghost of fun wraps 'round and shines,
In sticky notes and scribbled lines.
Loneliness in jests so sweet,
Companions hide in small defeats.

In the silence, a joke emerges,
Tickling thoughts as humor surges.
Alone we giggle, solo we play,
With solitude dancing, come what may.

Quiet Reveries

In silent dreams, the fun begins,
As dust motes spin, the laughter wins.
A chair reclines with playful flair,
Whispering secrets through the air.

The fridge hums softly, does a jig,
While forgotten food starts playing big.
Each cupcake's laugh is sweet and bold,
With icing secrets yet untold.

Window panes catch the sun's delight,
As shadows stretch and take their flight.
A sneeze erupts, a startled puff,
What fun can come from being rough!

In the corners, light beams tease,
Collecting giggles with greatest ease.
Quiet reveries share their mirth,
With each small moment full of worth.

Secrets in the Stillness

Whispers echo in the air,
A cat's meow, the chair's old squeak.
Chocolate hidden everywhere,
But the dog is far too meek.

Crumbs are counting like small sheep,
Ants are marching in a row.
In my dreams, I might just leap,
Over cushions just to glow.

Hiding from a tickled breeze,
Dust bunnies dance like high school bands.
Socks and slippers come with ease,
Tripping, falling, caught unplanned.

Giggles weave through afternoon,
With a book stacked on my head.
Surprises burst like cheerful tunes,
In my own little homestead.

Nature's Quiet Heartbeat

The garden gnomes have secret chats,
While pests debate the night's best feast.
Worms in bow ties, while the bats,
Steal snacks, chirping like a beast.

Bees wear sunglasses on their flight,
As daisies wiggle with a twist.
The moon peeks in, a funny sight,
Holding jokes in nature's mist.

Crickets croon their nightly songs,
The frogs reply in bass so deep.
Laughter flows where life belongs,
While nighttime wraps us in its sleep.

Starlight twinkles in delight,
Fireflies dance with sparks of joy.
Every shadow feels just right,
Nothing can this fun destroy.

Traces of Lives Lived

Scattered toys from days gone by,
Left behind with just a grin.
Old photo albums tell a lie,
Where silly faces surely win.

Balloons float up—who let them go?
The answer hides in coffee grounds.
Midday naps in sun's soft glow,
Are competitions for our hounds.

Popcorn kernels mark the seats,
Of movie nights that made us cheer.
A stubborn sock that never meets,
Its pair—oh, how it brings us near!

We laugh at all the twisty bends,
The echoes of our busy pace.
In quiet spaces, friendship blends,
Finding joy with every trace.

The Space Between Thoughts

What if my coffee cup could talk?
It'd spill secrets, surely bold.
And why do socks just up and walk?
There's tales of chaos to be told.

The chair holds whispers, light as air,
While dust collects in cheeky piles.
Moments linger, without a care,
Even the clock just plays in styles.

Ideas bounce, like balls on walls,
Sketching dreams in vibrant hues.
Tickled by silence, laughter calls,
In corners where the day renews.

Teapots sing of days gone past,
Each flip of pages holds a grin.
In the quiet, joy will last,
As thoughts waltz softly, deep within.

Timeless Secrets of the Unseen

In shadows lurk the sock you lost,
And whispers hide the dust you tossed.
The cat declares its reign today,
While robots practice ballet play.

Old books smile, sharing tales of yore,
They laugh at vacuum's every roar.
The clock ticks loud, it thinks it's sly,
But we prefer the nap nearby.

Things that giggle out of sight,
A curtain flutters—such delight!
The fridge hums tunes of yesterday,
As biscuits bribe with buttery sway.

In corners, chairs conspire and scheme,
While plants plot their next daring dream.
The tea kettle sings its playful tune,
As cookies dance upon the moon.

Calmness Cradled in Wood and Stone

Beneath the table, treasures lie,
A crayon hat, a rogue butterfly.
The chair squeaks gossip from the floor,
As silence begs for just one roar.

A light bulb flickers like it knows,
To keep interiors on their toes.
In quiet corners, squishy things,
Share tales of love and chair swing flings.

A sleepy dog and cat parade,
Their grandeur speaks, yet is dismayed.
The clock strikes hours in jest and laughs,
While dust mites settle their signed autographs.

Mismatched socks in harmony,
They launch a coup, no one agrees.
The sofa snores, it's quite absurd,
Yet laughter echoes—every word.

Beneath the Canopy of Quietude

In shadows, secrets like to dwell,
A peanut steals a nutty spell.
The rug composes symphonies,
While lamps wink with mischief, oh please!

The window sighs, it's had enough,
While curtains play peek-a-boo tough.
The woodwork creaks like it's alive,
Counting stories that still thrive.

Pet rocks whisper secrets sublime,
As clock hands dance in silly mime.
The pantry holds its laughter tight,
Content with crumbs that feel just right.

Behind each whisper, giggles bloom,
As daylight fades into the room.
A laughter echo, soft and wild,
These quiet walls, like a playful child.

Moments Suspended in Gentle Stillness

A spider spins its thread of dreams,
While sunlight dances, bright and beams.
The carpet's tales will never end,
With napping cushions as a friend.

The echo of a sneeze turns loud,
A pet's discourse bursts through the crowd.
The picture frames all try to grin,
As memories waltz, thick and thin.

An old shoe sings of dances bold,
While dust bunnies plot stories untold.
The fridge's hum is out of tune,
Yet it could play for a lazy moon.

Echoes soft and sweetly loud,
In playful chaos, we're allowed.
A moment caught, serene and swift,
These places hold our subtle gift.

The Timelessness of Muffled Hearts

In a room where whispers play,
The clock forgot to mark the day.
A sock is missing, no surprise,
It's hiding well—oh, crafty lies.

The cat's on guard, with watchful paws,
He plots the schemes with great applause.
The crumbs parade across the floor,
A hidden feast, who could want more?

Laughter echoes off the beams,
As silly thoughts spill into dreams.
A chair that squeaks, a funny tune,
We dance, we trip, beneath the moon.

In this scene of quiet cheer,
Time's a clown, it holds us near.
With every giggle, hearts do race,
In laughter's glow, we find our place.

Solitude Wrapped in Warmth

A blanket hug, the sofa's soft,
A dance with dust that floats aloft.
The kettle's whistle, tea to brew,
It sings of joy, how about you?

The fridge hums tales of bygone meals,
With pickles lost, it sadly feels.
A lonely spoon, a fork's regret,
Together they dream, it's quite a pet.

The shelves hold books with tales too grand,
A world of mischief at my hand.
I giggle at a character's fate,
A hero's blunder—how first-rate!

In cozy corners, time won't flee,
Mirth fills the air, it's just for me.
Wrapped in warmth, solitude's song,
We laugh at quiet; it won't be long.

The Blessing of Quiet Days

A lazy afternoon with tea,
Sunbeams dance playfully with me.
The toaster pops some bread so bright,
It startled me—a funny sight!

A squirrel taps against the glass,
With tiny paws, he plots and laughs.
He hoards his snacks, a crafty thief,
The sight of him brings disbelief.

The pillow fights from last week's fling,
A soft reminder that we sing.
With imaginary duels and jests,
Who knew such silence could be best?

Each moment treasured, laughter spills,
In cozy nooks, a heart just thrills.
Quiet days are a playful tease,
Unraveled joy, oh, what a breeze!

Where Time Stands Still

A grandfather clock with a sleepy yawn,
It's missed the show; the hours are gone.
Dust bunnies scurry, a fluffy crew,
While I sip coffee—a lively brew.

The neighbors argue, cats jump high,
A comedy show beneath the sky.
With every peep from window's frame,
Each shout and laugh, it's all the same.

A game of cards, and someone's cheat,
We all pretend to take defeat.
Chips fall like leaves, what a mess,
In giggles wrapped, we find our bliss.

Here laughter lives, and time's a prank,
In pauses where our joys create.
When stillness reigns, it makes us smile,
Where time stands still, we linger awhile.

Stories Lingering in Shadows

Dust bunnies host a dance,
Twilight's glow, a last romance.
Footsteps echo, a sock's escape,
Whispers laugh, a hidden shape.

Old chairs creak with tales untold,
Of mischief wide, and children bold.
The fridge hums a sleepy tune,
As mice compose a midnight swoon.

Glasses clink, ghosts toast their fame,
With every sound, they stake their claim.
Sofa cushions, a mountain trail,
Adventures fixed in silence pale.

Oh, the stories that unfold,
In corners lace, where dreams are sold.
Giggles stir from curtains drawn,
In shadows' play, the night's a fawn.

Reverberations of the Unsaid

A clock ticks laughter, time's sweet jest,
With every tick, it takes a rest.
Muffled secrets tickle the air,
Echoes bounce, no need for flair.

Worn-out shoes hang on the wall,
Dreams of dancing, but would they fall?
Plant pots gossip in leafy sighs,
While curtains plot with knowing eyes.

The wind chimes gossip, clang, and ring,
As if they're friends in a silly fling.
Beneath the stairs, a cat lays low,
Pretending to mind the world's goofy show.

Whispers trill, the night is bright,
With echoes of laughter that take flight.
In every nook, a chuckle hums,
With silent stories, the humor thrums.

The Quietude of Abandoned Places

In the attic, hats have fun,
Dancing as the day is done.
Old dolls play poker on the floor,
Laughing at the ghostly lore.

Walls adorned with cobweb lace,
Holding tales of a frantic race.
Boxes whisper of dreams mislaid,
While dust bunnies perfectly parade.

The old piano hums a tune,
Of cats and kings beneath the moon.
Mice join in with their own beat,
In this quiet space, they're quite the feat.

With every creak, a chuckle flows,
In this chamber, the humor grows.
Memories dance in silent waltz,
As laughter echoes, never halts.

Frames of Stillness

In a framed picture, a cat grins wide,
While the dog next to her seems to hide.
Clock hands pause to catch their breath,
As the chairs reminisce of warmth and depth.

Paintings wink from the wall with pride,
Bears in bow ties, a funny guide.
Books on the shelf giggle in rhyme,
Adventures silent, waiting for time.

Curtains twitch like a shy little friend,
Spying on moments that never end.
Birds outside create a ruckus anew,
While walls chuckle at all they knew.

Each corner holds a chuckling tale,
Of socks that travel and ships that sail.
In frames of stillness, there's so much fun,
As life, in silence, has just begun.

Solitude's Embrace

In corners where shadows play,
I sip my tea, quite far away.
The cat stares back, with eyes that gleam,
His judgment loud, or so it seems.

I dance with dust, a solo show,
In slippers soft, I feel the flow.
The walls might echo my little prance,
And yet I find, they join the dance.

A sock appears, gone from its mate,
I toss it high, it meets its fate.
The clock ticks on, it takes a pause,
Claustrophobic? Nah, just because.

With walls that watch, they hold my jest,
They listen well, they know me best.
In solitude, I find my cheer,
These funny bones, they linger here.

Ghosts of Laughter Past

In memories stored like dusty books,
A ghostly laugh? Just take a look!
I chuckle loud, they laugh right back,
A crew of jesters in my pack.

Their faces fade but jokes remain,
Like echoes in a playful chain.
They gather round, with mischievous glee,
In silence cast, they still joke with me.

One tickles the past with slight surprise,
As I recall those bright, bold ties.
Laughter ghosting in the halls,
A symphony of old, my laughter calls.

So here I sit, a hapless host,
To ghosts who laugh and love the most.
In every whisper, there's a grin,
A haunted place where joy begins.

The Weight of Unsaid Words

Between the breaths, a silence weighs,
Unsaid thoughts march in wild displays.
With puns and whispers trapped in air,
They twirl around, a jester's dare.

Should I express the things I feel,
Or sit in jest, a comic reel?
The weight of words, a heavy load,
Yet laughter shines on this grey road.

A wink can shout what words can't say,
A chuckle brightens up the day.
The tension cracks like summer heat,
In laughter's arms, we find our beat.

So here I sit, tongue tied and bold,
In quiet jest, the truth unfolds.
The weight of laughter shared, not lost,
In unsaid words, we pay the cost.

Stillness Speaks Louder

In stillness, where the humor lies,
The silence giggles, soft surprise.
A raised eyebrow, a knowing glance,
In quietude, we join the dance.

The walls stand tall, like silent friends,
In hushed amusement, laughter bends.
Shadows snicker, the floorboards creak,
In this calm, it's joy we seek.

Time squeaks by in moments slow,
With quiet chuckles, feelings flow.
An awkward pause, a sudden grin,
In stillness deep, the fun begins.

So let us dwell where laughter plays,
In still, sweet moments, brightened days.
With quiet walls and echoes mild,
The funny linger, blissfully wild.

Whispered Secrets in the Twilight

A cat with a hat and a pair of shoes,
Chasing shadows, singing the blues.
Whispers echo, a playful parade,
Where laughter drifts, and worries fade.

Beneath the moon's mischievous wink,
Jokes unfold faster than you can think.
A squirrel in stripes steals the last bite,
Making a dash, oh what a sight!

Giggling trees share their wildest dreams,
While owls exchange their wittiest schemes.
The air is thick with giggles and glee,
In this twilight dance, just let it be.

The stars peek out, brimming with jests,
As night attire puts the day to rest.
In whispered secrets, joy takes flight,
In a world so silly, everything's bright.

Threads of Stillness Intertwined

On a chilly morn, the socks refuse,
To match or pair, they seem to choose.
A dance of laundry, the clothespins sway,
Tickling the breeze in their own ballet.

A spider spins tales, with glee and flair,
While the dust bunnies plot in their lair.
Under the bed, they have their own ball,
Decked in lost socks, they have a ball.

The clock giggles, tick-tock with sass,
As time tumbles by, then races past.
In the quiet corners of this delight,
Every little moment feels just right.

The sun peeks in, ready to shine,
On shenanigans sweet, almost divine.
And laughter filigrees through the day,
In threads of joy, we dance and play.

The Sanctuary of Softly Falling Leaves

Breezy whispers, a pause for thought,
A leaf falls down, 'What a ride I've sought!'
Wiggly worms giggle, dance on the ground,
Over stones and twigs, they're silly and profound.

A raccoon, bemused, wears a chef's hat,
Declaring, 'Dinner! Let's feast, how about that?'
But his friends all laugh, 'Just scraps, my dear!'
In the wrinkled shadows, they have no fear.

Acorns tumble, rolling away,
Squirrels in their nutty ballet.
They chat with the birds in a playful tone,
In a sanctuary built of giggles and stone.

The breeze carries echoes of jocular things,
As nature hums and gently sings.
In soft, falling leaves, joys come alive,
In a sanctuary where smiles thrive.

Embraced by the Silence of Ages

In a corner, a chair creaks with mirth,
Eager to share the best of its worth.
It holds ancient tales of joy and woe,
Of socks that vanish, and seeds that grow.

The dusty books beckon with a grin,
Hiding the stories of what's within.
With every page turned, whispers delight,
As secrets are freed into the night.

Ghostly giggles flutter through the air,
An echo of mischief, a bold little dare.
In shadows where smoky tales gently stir,
The silence chuckles, it's never a blur.

A tapestry woven of laughter and light,
Floating through ages, forever in sight.
In every quiet nook, a joke is spun,
Chasing the silence, a whimsical run.

Echoes of Stillness

In corners where the dust bunnies play,
The echo of laughter escapes in the day.
Tickling the rafters, the whispers collide,
Until curtains are dancing, no need to hide.

A sock that is missing from under the bed,
Has given the cat a new throne in my head.
The fridge hums a tune, a jolly old song,
While I try to remember where I went wrong.

The plants chat with shadows, gossiping loud,
While I sit with my coffee, feeling so proud.
Old chairs creak and chuckle, a riotous spree,
As the quietness hides, oh, such glee to be free.

In the attic the ghosts are just cleaning up,
They brew ghostly tea in a chipped paper cup.
With each little creak, they take turns to tease,
Keeping the stillness in stitches with ease.

Whispers Between the Bricks

Two mice in the pantry begin to conspire,
Planning a feast, they plot and aspire.
They giggle and scamper, no worries or cares,
While the cat snoozes on, dreaming of lairs.

A wall flower blooms, right next to a crack,
Reminds me of my roommate who won't take a snack.
"Call me" it whispers, "when hunger does strike,"
While I munch on a cookie and grab me a pint.

The shadows play peek-a-boo, flickering light,
The wallpaper blushes with rumors of fright.
A spork on the table, a noodle in sight,
It's a dinner party, let's add some delight!

Cobwebs are weaving a tale full of jest,
The dust gathers secrets, it's really a fest.
Between bricks and mortar, the laughter will swell,
Turning the quiet into a whimsical spell.

Secrets Within the Silence

On a shelf of old trinkets, a rubber band sings,
Of the days gone by and precarious things.
A record that skips has a story to tell,
Of the dances we had, and the falls as well.

A dust mote takes flight, like a dragon on cue,
While the vacuum awaits, with its menacing hue.
I dodge and I weave as it roars through the hall,
And the laughter erupts from the paintings on the wall.

An empty wine bottle has visions to share,
Of nights spent with friends, and the gossip we dare.
While chairs tell of stories from long years ago,
Carving the silence with delight in their glow.

Within this house of whispers, joy finds its way,
Through laughter and echoes that dance and play.
Each secret that stirs in the stillness so bright,
Turns mundane to magic, transforming the night.

Shadows of Forgotten Hope

In corners where shadows think they can lurk,
A tickle of laughter reveals their true perk.
A lonely old broom stands guard at the door,
While the dust bunnies argue on chores and encore.

The fridge speaks in hums, a wise counselor known,
Recommending leftovers with a love once shown.
While plates stack their laughter, all teetering tall,
A game of unwitting, will someone just call?

An old shoe reclines; it's seen better days,
But it dreams of the dances — oh, glorious ways!
With paper and pencils, the shadows compose,
A symphony born from the quiet and prose.

Beneath all the stillness, a carnival brews,
As curtains engage in theatrical views.
The laughter erupts like a thunderous clap,
Turning silence to fun, in a fanciful trap.

Soft Footfalls on Silent Floors

Tiptoeing through the empty hall,
A sockless ghost is bound to fall.
The floorboards creak with silly glee,
As I dance alone, just me and me.

The cat gives me a puzzled look,
As I stumble, trip, and then just cook.
My sock is hiding, where could it be?
Oh, the life of a humorous spree.

A shadow leaps, a daring play,
In my own home, I am the ballet.
Twists and turns, my inner clown,
While my lonely slippers smile and frown.

With every creak, a new demand,
The ghosts in here must understand.
This is my stage, no audience near,
Just clumsy jigs that bring me cheer.

Traces of Light Through Gaps

Sunbeams peek through blinds askew,
Crafting patterns—look, there's a zoo!
The dust motes dance, they twist and twirl,
While I fumble my way through life's swirl.

A rogue ray strikes the cat's sleepy face,
She yawns, then stretches in her warm place.
What a show, the light steals the scene,
As I chase shadows with a wobbly grin.

A glimmer here, a glint over there,
It's a game of hide and seek—beware!
I stumble again, setting off my own fire,
A laugh escaped as I danced in the mire.

Caught in the trap of quirky delight,
The beams of sun become my spotlight.
With each flicker and silly fray,
I celebrate the warm, absurd display.

Reveries of the Whispering Breeze

The wind whispers secrets through the trees,
Tickling my ear with a friendly tease.
It beckons me to join its sly dance,
So I join in, without a second glance.

Floating papers up and away,
As I chase them, I tumble and sway.
The breeze laughs at my ragged chase,
While I trip on air, a clown in space.

Laughter lilts, the rafters all hum,
As I stumble over my thoughts undone.
What chaos spun inside my head?
A giggle erupts, by folly I'm led.

In this breeze, my worries dissolve,
With every gust, new problems evolve.
Yet, how funny, it all seems a jest,
As I dance with the wind, I find my rest.

Lurking in the Embrace of Shadows

The shadows huddle, plotting some schemes,
Casting giggles into my daydreams.
They wiggle and wriggle, a playful crowd,
In the dim light, they're silly and loud.

I tiptoe forward, in fear of a smirch,
The dark corners hold laughter's own perch.
With a wink and a grin, they beckon to play,
While I shy back, but I can't look away.

A thunderous whisper, a friendly call,
Inviting me deeper into the sprawl.
Here in the gloom, is that a funny face?
The shadows offer me laughter's embrace.

In this dim light, joy gets unbound,
With their charming antics, I follow the sound.
So here I remain, with shades of delight,
As I giggle and guffaw, in the soft night.

Faded Photographs and Forgotten Voices

In the attic, dust bunnies play,
Photographs fading, forgotten decay.
A smile captured in a frame,
Yet I can't remember their name.

Granny's hats piled up so high,
An uninvited spider winks an eye.
Old vinyl records spin with glee,
Singing tunes of who we used to be.

A box of letters, yellowed and frayed,
Stories of love in a word parade.
Each one signed with a funny quirk,
But who knew love was such hard work?

Ticking clocks and silly clocks,
Echoes of laughter and mismatched socks.
Who knew the past could be so bright?
In forgotten corners, we reignite.

The Ghosts of Unsung Laments

In dusty corners, shadows dance,
Phantom whispers of missed romance.
A ghost in socks takes off in flight,
But trip on a table, oh what a sight!

The wall paint peels like old cheese,
Fables told over cups of tease.
'Who's this ghost?' an echo jeers,
'Popcorn and soda, it's all my fears!'

In the cupboard, a pot turns green,
Maybe the ghost needs a cuisine routine.
But how can he cook with no hands?
A culinary dream in ghostly lands?

When night falls, they giggle and sway,
Haunting snacks that go astray.
With laughter bubbling in the air,
Ghosts of unsung laments declare.

Echoes Wandering Through Forgotten Halls

Echoes whisper down the hallway,
Hiding secrets from yesterday.
A lonely sock peeks round the bend,
Will it meet its long-lost friend?

Pictures of cats all dressed in style,
Make me chuckle, they linger awhile.
Their narrowed eyes and fuzzy tails,
Mimicking life like whimsical trails.

In the library, books stacked high,
Dusty tomes send clouds to the sky.
With each turn of the worn-out leaf,
Characters giggle, beyond belief.

Leftover popcorn from movie nights,
Traces of laughter in silly sights.
Old echoes tease, they know the score,
Wandering through, they ask for more!

A Tapestry of Stillness

A tapestry hung, stitched with care,
Adventurous stories float in the air.
Grandpa's tales, full of glee,
A yarn spun of mischief and tea.

In corners, cobwebs weave their threads,
While old curtains hide unmatched beds.
The rocking chair's charming creak,
As if it's showing some ancient sneak.

Socks mismatched, thinking they're chic,
A wardrobe full of laughter, unique.
Each garment holds a laugh or two,
As if they're pondering what one must do.

This stillness isn't all that it seems,
Filled with echoes of childhood dreams.
A canvas of moments hangs on the wall,
Quirky and merry, they beckon us all.

The Stories Etched in Silence

In corners where dust loves to dance,
A chair squeaks like it's got a chance.
Whispers of socks that have gone astray,
They giggle at shoes that can't find their way.

Chairs tell tales of a snack attack,
Where crumbs are kings, and mice have a knack.
The old clock laughs at our hurried woes,
Ticking away while no one quite knows.

A picture hangs crooked, a familiar face,
It winks like it knows we're in a race.
With laughter echoing off the walls,
These stories just bounce, not caught in their thralls.

Through silence we find our delight,
In tales of the past that take flight.
Not a soul around to hear us plead,
Yet the walls are alive with laughter indeed.

Solace in the Forgotten Nooks

In the back of the room where the dust bunnies play,
Couches conspire to steal the day.
A forgotten shoe sports a cozy heel,
While the cat rolls by in a casual reel.

The lamp thinks it's a star in disguise,
Flashing bright at its own silly lies.
Old books chuckle with stories undone,
Hiding their secrets from everyone.

Quirky knick-knacks that gather the light,
Each one is ready to share a good fright.
When no one is watching, they start to confide,
Jokes that float freely, they can't abide.

In silence we find a mirthful embrace,
With whimsy that twirls at its own steady pace.
Here's a toast to the quiet, so loudly it calls,
In the forgotten nooks where laughter sprawls.

The Unseen Guardian of Tranquility

A shadow with scissors that snip at the air,
Cleans up the mess of a scattered despair.
It snickers at chaos with glee in its heart,
As laughter erupts when the socks fall apart.

A guardian lurking in plain sight and sound,
Tending to mayhem where joy is unbound.
The fridge hums softly a sweet little tune,
While leftover pizzas are lost in the moon.

The rug hides the secrets of birthdays gone wild,
It absorbs all the giggles as laughter beguiled.
A wink from the window, a nudge from the floor,
Each nook and each cranny is hiding some more.

With mischief and whispers, it calls us to play,
In the light of the silliness here every day.
A warm laugh embraces the oddities sworn,
In the arms of the unseen, we're all newly born.

Nightfall's Gentle Caress

As dusk tiptoes in on its tiptoed toes,
The curtains get cozy, and the sill gently doze.
Mugs filled with giggles are set on the shelf,
While pillows conspire to snicker themselves.

Moonlight sneaks in through a crack in the frame,
It dances with shadows, it revels in fame.
Whispers of dreams come in for a rest,
While pajamas declare they're truly the best.

The lamp tells a story of light without fright,
As the clock keeps on chuckling throughout the night.
Beneath all the chuckles and soft lullabies,
Rest the secrets that cause us to rise.

Each tick and each tock holds a playful jest,
Bringing warmth to the quiet, we're truly blessed.
As nightfall's embrace makes the world soft and bare,
We find joy in the stillness, and laughter to spare.

The Secret Life of Walls

In corners where dust bunnies conspire,
Walls giggle, plotting their own grand choir.
They whisper tales of socks gone astray,
A runaway shoe and a cat's fine ballet.

They hold secret parties with wallpapered friends,
Where echoes of laughter and light never end.
With paint chips for confetti, they dance through the night,

As neighbors grumble, 'Why's it so bright?'

A crack in the plaster reveals a sly grin,
With a wink and a nod, say, 'Let the fun begin!'
When the moonlight comes dripping like butter on bread,
They'll toast with old keys that are better off dead.

So if you should listen when nighttime takes hold,
Just know the walls love to spin tales bold.
Each squeak of the floorboards, a comedic cue,
In the life of the walls, there's always a show to view.

Where Silence Sings

When silence creeps in like a cat in a hat,
Walls hum a tune both silly and fat.
With whispers of laughter and echoes of bliss,
They croon silly songs that you wouldn't want to miss.

The curtains will sway as they join in the fun,
While the chairs tap their toes, oh look, there's a pun!
A pillow starts chuckling, can you believe?
As dust motes take flight with great joy to conceive.

A duet of shadows skips 'cross the floor,
While lampshades gossip, what's behind that door?
As clocks stop to listen with hands poised in jest,
The night melts away—oh, what a wild fest!

So when it gets quiet and the world fades away,
Remember the walls play in their own merry way.
Let laughter resound as the silence takes wing,
In this symphony of stillness, where silence sings.

Beneath the Weight of Quiet Dreams

Beneath dream-laden beams that hold up the night,
Walls dream of kittens in capes ready to fight.
With thoughts of old socks and odd little toys,
They giggle together, those resilient joys.

In a slumbering dance, they cradle the lore,
Of forgotten adventures behind every door.
A fridge humming softly, a gentle old croon,
While the cabinets boogie beneath the full moon.

When morning arrives with giggles and yawns,
The walls put away all their whimsical fawns.
They brace for the chaos of waking lives call,
Yet they'll always find time for their dreams in the hall.

So join in the laughter; join in the scheme,
For life's a grand joke woven through every dream.
And beneath all that weight, when the workday redeems,
The walls will still chuckle, dressed in silken seams.

The Lull of Forgotten Futures

In shadows, they whisper the plans of the past,
Of great things unsaid and dreams that won't last.
Walls cradle the fables of futures sad,
While doors creak with laughter, recalling the bad.

A sneaky old paint chip reveals tales of yore,
As the floorboards giggle, 'We've seen this before!'
Each dent tells a story, a laugh or a shout,
In this world of the quiet, there's always a route.

Forgotten futures dance like dust in the light,
With walls rolling their eyes, so delightfully bright.
They've seen all the schemes we thought would come true,

Now wrapped in the comfort of an inside review.

So next time you ponder what might have been done,
Cast your gaze to the walls—they have laughs to be spun.

For in all of the futures that never took flight,
Lies a lull of funny in the depth of the night.

The Beauty of Unspoken Thoughts

Whispers dance in empty rooms,
Echoes laugh at silly grooms.
Thoughts that tickle, thoughts that tease,
Wrap them up in a gentle breeze.

Nods that say what words can't reach,
Like a fish that learned to breach.
Grins that flutter like a moth,
In the stillness, they find both.

Silly secrets in the light,
Hiding giggles, oh so bright.
Puns and jests in shadows seep,
A silent chuckle, deep and steep.

Jumbled meanings, pure delight,
Chasing laughter in the night.
Quiet corners share their cheer,
Unseen jokes, delightfully near.

Oaths of the Unseen

Promises linger in the air,
Mutual winks, a secret dare.
Sworn to silence, vows so bold,
Stories shared, but never told.

The corners giggle, the walls blush,
Whispered truths create a hush.
Oaths of laughter, joy concealed,
Silly antics, best revealed.

Tiny giggles, you hear them clear,
Catch them fast, for they disappear.
Muffled chuckles behind closed doors,
Comedic echoes, rich with roars.

Promises made to keep it light,
Ticklish moments, pure delight.
In the stillness, laughter lies,
A mischievous twinkle in our eyes.

Chasing the Silence

Hushed whispers and shifty glances,
In the stillness, laughter dances.
Chasing silence, it's quite a feat,
While hidden giggles take a seat.

A sly grin against the wall,
Echoes of snickers that softly call.
Tickles erupt from corners, unseen,
Swiping joy like it's a routine.

Sneaky chuckles, they bounce and thud,
As silence cradles a pillow of mud.
The walls giggle at the blunder,
In the quiet, we place our wonder.

So if you seek that playful sound,
Look for laughter that's tightly wound.
Chasing echoes, in circles we spin,
What our hearts skip, we always win.

Reverence for the Quiet Moments

In hushed tones, we bow and pray,
To the giggles that slip away.
Moments where silence has a flair,
Crafting joy that fills the air.

A pause for laughter, soft and grand,
Invisible antics, unplanned.
High fives of stillness, floating free,
Ticklish secrets between you and me.

Toasting to quiet, a comic jest,
Under the radar, where we rest.
Moments that slip between the lines,
A shared smile, where humor shines.

So here's to whispers that make us grin,
Celebrating where laughter begins.
In understated joy, we find our way,
Loving the quietness of each day.

Cadences of the Invisible

In the corners, whispers play,
Like cats who waltz on a sunny day.
They tiptoe round, avoid the cracks,
Their giggles echo, never relax.

A sock will dance, a shoe will prance,
Life's a party, it seems by chance.
Muffled laughter fills the space,
As dust bunnies join in the chase.

Invisible friends, they play their tune,
Singing softly beneath the moon.
Caught in a game, where shadows flit,
One roll of the dice, and they won't quit.

In the stillness, humor rests,
Beneath the quiet, laughter tests.
A riddle hidden in every grin,
What's velcro for, when laughter's the win?

The Breath Between Words

In a room where silence hums,
A misplaced laugh escapes and drums.
Between two pauses, awkward, the glow,
As if the walls are in on the show.

A chair that creaks like it knows a joke,
Echoes softly, while we both choke.
The clock ticks loudly, trying to blend,
With all of our awkwardness, we pretend.

The breath between letters, it holds its breath,
A punchline hidden beneath their heft.
Words wiggle free like playful fish,
While we moonwalk dance and make a wish.

In laughter's hold, a secret lies,
Between our murmurs and alibis.
A quirky air makes the mundane swirled,
Turning awkward moments into a world.

Soft Shadows of Longing

Beneath the light, shadows tease,
They laugh and dance, do as they please.
A longing sigh, a curvy stretch,
As wishes float just out of reach.

A blanket whispers soft and warm,
It cradles dreams in an unusual form.
The pillow giggles, caught in a sprawl,
While socks attempt a stand-up call.

Tickling breezes rustle the night,
As hopes play peekaboo, out of sight.
They trip on shadows, they laugh so loud,
In the dance of yearning, we all feel proud.

Though soft and sweet, love's a jester,
Wearing a crown with a comedic gesture.
We'll twirl in sighs, each wish a wing,
In this shadowy jig, hear the joy we bring.

Murmurs Lost in the Attic

Up in the attic, secrets unfold,
Murmurs and giggles, brave and bold.
A rocking chair, without a care,
Sways back and forth in the dusty air.

Boxes piled high, old stories sprout,
A forgotten toy softly shouts.
With each glance, nostalgia bites,
As laughter mingles with the old lights.

Cobwebs hang like curtains drawn,
Where silliness reigns from dusk till dawn.
A mouse wearing glasses reads the news,
While echoes dance in comic shoes.

Amidst the dusty beams, joy resides,
Tucked in the corners where memory hides.
With chuckles and whispers, they weave a tale,
In the attic's embrace, laughter prevails.

Cages of Contemplation

In the room where dust bunnies dance,
My thoughts take a silly chance.
A cat plays chess with a shoe,
While I ponder life's great stew.

A goldfish grins with knowing eyes,
As I search for my missing fries.
The walls giggle with each small creak,
In this haven where silence speaks.

Framed memories on the shelf,
Tell stories of my former self.
I laugh at the ghost in my chair,
Who shrugs at life's carousel fare.

With each tick of the old clock's hand,
I plot my escape to nowhere planned.
The echoes bend, they twist and shout,
In this cage, I'm right at home, no doubt.

Dialogues with the Echoes

Talking to shadows has its charm,
Especially when they mean no harm.
The fridge hums tunes of lost delights,
While I argue with the ceiling lights.

"Did you see that?" I ask the wall,
"Another daydream, or not at all?"
The echoes chuckle, a teasing lot,
Saying, "Your sanity? Let's just trot."

A sock puppet serves as my sage,
Dispensing wisdom from its cage.
We laugh at life's bizarre ballet,
As time waltzes in a funny way.

In whispers soft, they chirp and tease,
Practicing secrets with the breeze.
Conversations with cobwebs and dust,
In this theater of silly mistrust.

Reflections in the Void

A mirror stares with a comical frown,
"Is that really you?" it jests with a clown.
I nod back with hair like a bird's nest,
In this carnival, I'm truly blessed.

The clock jokes about time in a rush,
While I sit here, in a thoughtful hush.
A teapot giggles at my tea stains,
As I sift through my mental gain trains.

Pillow fights with my wildest thoughts,
Unraveling truths that life forgot.
I chuckle with candles, flickering bright,
As day reveals its quirky delight.

A wild dance of echoes and glee,
In a space where the void holds the key.
I twirl with my shadows, what fun we make,
In this oddball adventure, no one's awake.

The Solitary Sanctuary

Here in my nest of mismatched socks,
The walls confide, unlock silly locks.
An army of mugs watches me plot,
As I scheme with a loaf of bread, quite hot.

The sofa's a throne for the whims of day,
Where I ponder the meaning of "okay."
With pillows to guard my wacky schemes,
I throw confetti into my dreams.

The dust motes waltz, a cavalcade,
Laughing at the sock puppet parade.
Calendar pages flutter and dance,
In this fortress of nonsense, I prance.

With cookies as allies, I plan a feast,
In this sanctuary, I'm never the least.
What fun we conjure within these four walls,
In my strange little haven, laughter enthralls.

Unraveled Threads of Time

Tick-tock goes the clock, without a care,
My socks mismatched, oh, the laundry's a flare!
Coffee stains dance on the ancient wood,
I swear it was clean, once, if only it could.

Dust bunnies leap, as the vacuum I chase,
They laugh at my struggles, oh, what a disgrace!
A family of crumbs on the couch takes a seat,
Sometimes they party, who knew they'd be neat?

Forgotten leftovers, a science fair prize,
They wave as I pass, with their greenish eyes.
Who knew food could rally with such a strong will?
I tiptoe away, lest they say, "Let's chill!"

Each day a new2 rap battle with socks,
Off to the laundry, dodging tick-tock rocks.
But through all the chaos and comical plight,
I'll wear stripes and polka dots, and call it all right!

The Peace of Empty Rooms

A chair sits vacant, it's quite the lone scene,
Dust dances in sunlight, so regal and clean.
I swear it just whispered, 'Get off of my rug!'
"Fine," I responded, "I'll give you a hug!"

The fridge hums a tune, quite an odd serenade,
As I rummage for snacks, it's the song of my trade.
Peanut butter winks, while my apples roll by,
So I raise up a toast to the wonders nearby!

An empty vase tells tales of flowers long gone,
I picture their laughter—oh, what a sweet con!
The sofa holds secrets of naps taken still,
While the clock laughs loudly, "Time waits for no thrill!"

In corners of silence, my thoughts run around,
They trip over echoes, a soft silly sound.
So here's to the quiet, the peace that it brings,
In my empty rooms, every odd moment sings!

Whispers of Stillness

A quiet room hums like a secretive tune,
Where shadows plot mischief, or maybe a swoon.
The curtains have secrets, they know every tale,
And the rug starts to laugh as I dance without fail.

Half-empty teacups hold the gossip of mugs,
While the cat casts a glance like a king with no thugs.
"Here comes the human," I swear I heard him purr,
"What's in that bag? Could it be more fur?"

A pair of old mittens play tag by the door,
While cobwebs in corners are planning a score.
"Phantom of socks!" I declare with a grin,
But the laundry's my nemesis, where do I begin?

They whisper and giggle, those ghosts of my past,
As I trip on their tales, each memory cast.
In the stillness, there's laughter, trust me, it's real,
Life's too short for silence—it's joy we should steal!

Shadows Beneath the Eaves

Shadows scamper, a game of hide and seek,
They giggle behind corners, so cheeky and sleek.
Dust motes float by, like tiny confetti,
As I trip in my slippers, oh, isn't life petty?

The teapot whistles, a curious alarm,
"Your tea's getting cold, come quick, don't you charm!"
But I wander and ponder; is it fun or mere fate?
I dance with the shadows, they say, "You're our mate!"

The wallpaper peels back, a laugh from the past,
With its floral delights, cheerfully cast.
It chuckles at memories of parties long gone,
Funny hats perched on friends singing along.

So here I sit, with a rich, silly stew,
In this laughter of time, friendships feel new.
The shadows, they wink, as I clink my old cup,
Here's to the moments, when we laugh and erupt!

Murmurs in the Abandoned Room

In a room where echoes play,
Dusty whispers dance all day.
A chair wobbles, creaks with glee,
Its laughter fills the void, you see.

A ghostly cat naps on the floor,
Dreaming of mice that are no more.
Forgotten toys in corners hide,
Waiting for a friend to slide.

A shadow peeks around the door,
It's probably just a broom, no more.
With a sigh, the light bulb flicks,
Lighting up the room's old tricks.

In corners, secrets lie awake,
Like lost socks in a laundry quake.
They giggle softly, oh so slight,
In this abandoned room of light.

Still Air

The air is thick with quiet fun,
As time tick-tocks, it's never done.
A fly buzzes, holding court,
On a wall that's far from sport.

The clock is stuck, it lost the race,
To find a funny little place.
A spider knits his web with flair,
Sparking laughter in the still air.

A sneeze from dust, a ghostly giggle,
Rattles the room with a tiny wiggle.
Old shoes laugh, thrown in a pile,
Telling tales with dust and style.

Moths flutter in their nightly cloak,
Plotting mischief, sharing a joke.
Though silence reigns, it's far from drab,
In still air, life's little jabs.

Unearthed Dreams

When I delve through old chests stored,
I find some dreams that once were adored.
A teddy bear with one eye,
Whispers secrets from days gone by.

A rubber band and a crumpled map,
Both play tag with a forgotten cap.
In the depths lie sighs and schemes,
Each item bursts with laughter's beams.

A diary with a lock gone loose,
Shares tales of crushes and wild moose.
Old love letters, torn and bent,
Send giggles scurrying, merriment lent.

Unearthed dreams in each dusty nook,
Are treasures hiding in every book.
A forgotten world of joy and cheer,
Crafted whispers that linger near.

Glistening Dust in Sunbeams

Sunlight spills through the window wide,
Kissing dust motes that softly glide.
They twirl in rays like little sprites,
Waging wars on the mellow nights.

A dancing lamp lampoons the floor,
Casting shadows that beg for more.
Each shimmered fleck holds a tale,
Of sock puppets and pirate sails.

The corners grin with dusty pride,
As the sunlight takes them for a ride.
With every flicker, laughter blooms,
In the glistening that softly looms.

Around the room, the echoes cry,
Whispers giggle as they fly.
A symphony of quiet glee,
In every sparkling, dancing tree.

The Calm Between the Storms

Before the storm, the world feels strange,
Like socks that wander, seeking change.
A squirrel ponders, high on a beam,
Plotting mischief, living the dream.

The kettle hums a gentle tune,
While spoons giggle, lining up in a swoon.
A chair winks, with a nod, it boasts,
About the time it hosted ghosts.

Outside, wind waits, in playful tune,
As clouds gather, they'll sing soon.
But in this moment, laughter reigns,
Amidst the wait, where silliness gains.

The calm invites antics all around,
With memories of silliness abound.
In every pause, a joke unfurls,
In this fleeting gap, life swirls.

Veil of Tranquil Moments

Whispers dance like sneaky cats,
Tickling minds with playful chats.
A squirrel scolds a car tire's plight,
As shadowed giggles steal the night.

Breezes drift with jokes untold,
As sunbeams shimmer, bold and gold.
A bird sings flat, yet claims it's sweet,
While squirrels plot a nutty feat.

Calm within this jesting space,
Where laughter takes a slow, warm pace.
The clock's a joker, won't define,
When time will stop to sip some wine.

Echo of a chuckle, light and spry,
Painted on the dimming sky.
In perfect stillness, oddities bloom,
A waltz of whimsy fills the room.

Silenced Echoes of Yesteryear

A chair creaks with a ghostly prance,
As memories invite to dance.
Old shoes sit with dusty flair,
Wondering who will dare to wear.

Curtains flutter with tales well-spun,
As shadows giggle in the sun.
The past is a clown, dressed in sass,
Making faces from polished glass.

Tick-tock of time plays hide and seek,
With laughter spilled upon each peak.
Footsteps hush in the cool, crisp air,
A comedy show with no one there.

In corridors where echoes roam,
Each whispered joke finds its home.
Silenced giggles beneath the years,
Turn memories into chuckled cheers.

Beneath Layers of Time

Dusty books with tales to share,
Giggle with whispers, light as air.
Each page a jest from days gone by,
With winks and nods, they flutter by.

A forgotten sock plays peek-a-boo,
In closets where secrets brew.
Chairs swap gossip, wooden and old,
While half-empty glasses laugh, bold.

Cobwebs weave a silken tale,
Of mouse-sized dramas that never pale.
Echoes linger in all they touch,
With tickles that don't ask for much.

Unlocked corners of silence deep,
Hum with chuckles that never sleep.
Layers peel, revealing laughter bright,
As history bows to humor's light.

The Unheard Lullaby

Crickets hum their off-key tune,
As the moon rolls by, a hefty boon.
Stars giggle with a twinkling sigh,
Spinning tales as night drifts high.

Frogs debate who croaks the best,
In a contest only they can jest.
A sleepy breeze, it shushes loud,
While whims roam free, unchained, proud.

Walls cradle secrets, worn and sweet,
While laughter spills from worn-out feet.
An unheard song floats through the air,
Wrapped in silliness, everywhere.

So close your eyes, let jesters sway,
In this dreamland, come what may.
For in the night, where whispers play,
The unheard lullaby finds its way.

www.ingramcontent.com/pod-product-compliance
Lightning Source LLC
Chambersburg PA
CBHW070007300426
43661CB00141B/270